SCHIRMER'S LIBRARY OF MUSICAL CLASSICS

B. LÜTGEN

Vocalises

Vol. I

TWENTY DAILY EXERCISES

→ High Voice — Library Vol. 654

Medium Voice — Library Vol. 655

Low Voice — Library Vol. 656

Vol. II

TWENTY OPERATIC VOCALISES

High Voice — Library Vol. 930

Low Voice — Library Vol. 931

Edited by

MAX SPICKER

G. SCHIRMER, Inc.

DISTRIBUTED BY

HAL•LEONARD®
CORPORATION

7777 W. BLUEMOUND RD. P.O. BOX 13819 MILWAUKEE, WI 53213

PREFACE.

The aim of these Vocalises is to render the voice sufficiently flexible and mellow to execute easily and elegantly the *colorature* and embellishments found in the works of our great composers. They are intended to be, for the singer, what Czerny's school of Velocity is for the pianist.

Proceeding from the principle, that it is unpractical to practise a variety of difficult passages at the same time, I begin with exercises on two, three, and four tones, then advancing progressively to more difficult exercises; leaving it to the teacher to transpose them a semitone higher or lower.

However, in order to avoid the monotony and lassitude which are almost inseparable from a strictly methodic course of study, I have endeavored to clothe my exercises in a musical and agreeable form; and have made them very short, to prevent overexertion of the voice.

Following its avowed purpose, this work contains no exercises for sustained tones; and it will suffice to sing daily a few long-sustained tones, before taking up these exercises.

The results obtained with this method, and its approbation by several of the highest musical authorities, justify my hope, that it will find a favorable reception.

B. LÜTGEN.

16084

Daily Exercises.

B. LÜTGEN.

Note. These vocal exercises may be gradually transposed a semitone higher or lower, without over-passing the natural limits of the voice.

✛) A like "a" in "father."

Note. After thoroughly practising these vocal exercises as they are written, the student may substitute thirty-second-notes for the sixteenth-notes.

8

*) half-breath.

Allegro giusto.

17.

Andante espressivo.

18.

Allegro moderato.

19.

Andante.

20.